All Shook Up

All Shook Up

The Little Book of Parkinson's Poetry

SUE HAMMOND

Copyright © 2019 by Sue Hammond.

ISBN: Softcover   978-1-5434-9441-9
         eBook   978-1-5434-9442-6

All rights reserved. No part of this book may be reproduced or transmitted in any form or by any means, electronic or mechanical, including photocopying, recording, or by any information storage and retrieval system, without permission in writing from the copyright owner.

This is a work of fiction. Names, characters, places and incidents either are the product of the author's imagination or are used fictitiously, and any resemblance to any actual persons, living or dead, events, or locales is entirely coincidental.

Any people depicted in stock imagery provided by Getty Images are models, and such images are being used for illustrative purposes only.
Certain stock imagery © Getty Images.

Print information available on the last page.

Rev. date: 01/31/2019

To order additional copies of this book, contact:
Xlibris
800-056-3182
www.Xlibrispublishing.co.uk
Orders@Xlibrispublishing.co.uk
790775

Contents

Foreword ix
Introduction Poem xi

Parkinson's poems By Sue Hammond

1. Just Diagnosed 1
2. I'm still me 2
3. The journey 4
4. PD Sound of Silence 6
5. Three years ago 8
6. It's time to go 9
7. The Demons come at night 10
8. Betty Blue 12
9. Pd just keeps giving 13
10. Where's our shining knight? 14
11. My Brain 15
12. Did I sleep? I forget 16
13. Please don't judge 17
14. Uninvited Guests 18
15. Will I still be me? 19
16. Pd I'm all shook up 20
17. Dementia 22

Miscellaneous Poetry 23

18. Happy New Year 24
19. Glasses and Pen 26
20. Exciting and new 28
21. The lake shore 30
22. The Menagerie 31

Parkinson's Poetry & Miscellaneous 33

    23 Today I Cried For Me 34
    24 Unwelcome Friend 36
    25 No Angels Today 38
    26 You Thief 40
    27 I'm Still Me 42
    28 Mr. Sandman 43
    29 Peppermint Gel 44
    30 Nobody's Phone 45
    31 Dark Clouds 46
    32 Caught 47
    33 Parkinson's 48
    34 Strictly Dancing On Thin Ice 49
    35 Ministry Of Shakes And Tremor 50
    36 Lonely 52
    37 Morning 53
    38 Despair In The Night 54
    39 Concluding Poem 55

Acknowledgements 56
Parkinson's UK Information 57

I would like to dedicate this book to my three son's
Craig, Scott and Simon who keep me strong.

Foreword

My name is Sue Hammond and I have Parkinson's. I wanted to produce this book to raise awareness and funding for the charity Parkinson's UK.

When I was first diagnosed in September 2015 I embarked on a journey of self-understanding and learning about the effect Parkinson's would have on my life.

There is a great release to be found in expressing oneself in poetry. These poems are often written during long sleepless nights when we only have our thoughts for company. Our local branch of Parkinson's UK offers a great source of information and support for those affected by this condition. One popular activity is a singing for fun group. Parkinson's affects the voice and facial muscles, and singing has a therapeutic benefit as well as being very enjoyable. I believe this triggered a stream of creativity which led to me writing poetry.

Hopefully reading these poems will give you an insight into this complex condition, and how it affects us both physically and emotionally.

There is no government funding for research and there have been no major breakthroughs with medication since the 1950s. We rely heavily on charities like Parkinson's UK to carry out their own studies as well as offering practical and emotional support through their helplines. This requires considerable financial investment. At the moment that all important cure is just out of reach.

There are many Parkinson's poets expressing their fears and experiences in the dead of night, I am proud to be one of them.

Thank you for purchasing our poems and getting our voices heard.

Introduction Poem

Our poems probably don't flow as you think they should
but please read on and let it be understood,
That Keats and Wordsworth we know we are not
but our writing is the only voice that we've got.
Our words are coming straight from the heart
I believe that is a good place for a poem to start

Our words will give you an insight into PD.
And we'll be glad to have some of your empathy.
We say "I'm still me" or "Will I still be me".
Because Parkinson's steals away our identity.
We fear that we will not be able to keep sane
that's because Parkinson's affects our brain

Medication can turn us into addicts or worse
Can change our personality and make us curse.
Our sleep will be stolen night after night.
Making us weak so that we struggle to fight.
We feel ashamed, our symptoms we'll try to hide.
Our poems are like having a good friend by our side

Fifty odd years for a cure we've had to wait.
It can't come too soon, for many it's already too late
So let me thank you for your time in taking a look
And know that the profits from the sales of this book,
Will help to bring us nearer to that elusive cure.
So no more Parkinson's we'll have to endure.

Thank you

Sue Hammond

Just Diagnosed

I can see that you struggle to comprehend.
How do you move forward? How do you mend?
Your old life is gone and the futures not clear.
But don't be afraid for I am here.

To know what was wrong, may at first be a relief,
But hard on its heels comes the despair and the grief.
What is to come? You'd rather not know.
But you'll be alright, so please don't get low.

You may worry about coping if you're disabled?
What if people put you in a box then have you labelled?
If you worry about the future it will drive you mad.
So live for today and be happy not sad.

I know where you are, I've walked in your shoes,
You will learn to accept, you have nothing to lose
Make the most of your time and enjoy life to the max
Only you can do it, these are the facts.

Life may get a bit rough and the going a bit tough.
But the ignorant you will learn to ignore.
So live for today and let the future find its way.
You still have your life to explore.

Sue Hammond

I'm still me

My muscles may ache and sometimes I'll shake.
I can struggle to stir my own tea.
So please be kind and open your mind,
Come closer to see the real me.
I am fighting this fight and I'm holding on tight.
But in the end it will be.
That while I'm alive I know I'll survive.
As deep inside, I'm still ME

My body feels old and my face may look cold.
You may struggle to relate to me
So please be kind and open your mind,
Come closer to see the real me.
I may seem a bit odd, like a drunken old sod.
I'm slurring but it's not really me.
So while I'm alive I know I'll survive.
As deep inside, I'm still ME

As my body moves slow, it is stiff and won't go.
I feel heavy and I cannot move free
So please be kind and open your mind,
Come closer to see the real me.
As I struggle to walk, some may struggle to talk.
I just hope that one doesn't get me.
So while I'm alive I know I'll survive.
As deep inside, I'm still ME

I shuffle, I stumble and often I tumble.
That's scary I think you'll agree
So please be kind and open your mind,
Come closer to see the real me.
When I can't sleep and I just want to weep,
The nightmares I just want to flee
But while I'm alive I will survive.
As deep inside I'm still me.

So as I advance you will see by my stance.
I can hide it no longer you see
So please be kind and open your mind.
Come closer to see the real me.
If I have to inject please show me some respect'
I'm not a junky you see.
And if I forget your name as I try to stay sane.
Just remember that I am still me

This Poem was put on Facebook and raised over £3000 for Unite for Parkinson's. It was also made into a song which can be found on YouTube. Just follow the links to see more.

www.facebook.com/uniteforparkinsons/videos/441674749604315
www.youtube.com/watch?=8Ay5G-n2Fhs

The journey

I saw a fortune teller when I was young,
It was just for a laugh, a bit of fun.
You'll go on a long journey the gypsy remarked.
You'll meet a stranger who will be tall and dark.
What a cliché, I bet she's told that one before.
Well that won't come true that's for sure.

But there was my stranger looking at me.
As he calmly announced "you have PD".
So the challenging journey had now begun.
My fate was sealed there was no place to run.
Knowledge was power I told myself
As I put my new pills upon the shelf.

The pills will keep the symptoms at bay.
I can pretend for a while that I'm okay.
Help could be found in many a book.
I'd be alright if all their advice I took.
If I keep a low profile no one will know.
So I'll pick myself up and off I'll go.

The pills then made me wiggle and dance.
I noticed I was getting the odd sideways glance.
I wanted to shout out that I have PD
But that would make it too real for me.
This journey was getting a little tough
I needed some help, I'd had enough.

I spoke to people who were in the same boat
Their stories helped me to not give up hope.
I'm still on my journey and learning things new.
But now have help from a strong sturdy crew.
We support each other as we journey along.
Because together we'll stand solid and strong.
I no longer have the urge to have my future foretold.
I don't need to see. I'm no longer that bold.

Sue Hammond

PD Sound of Silence

Hello PD you're no friend
You've came to stay until the end
You crept inside while I was sleeping
To take my freedom, leave me weeping.
Well listen because I'll fight you everyday,
All the way
Though it may be in silence

So inside me you will grow.
Stop me moving make me slow.
You steal my voice and you will steal my sleep
You'll make me tumble over my own feet
When the shaking starts, I must look an awful sight
This can't be right
So I will cry in the silence.

Fools said I, you do not know
The PD gets stronger as it grows
Hear my words so that I may teach you
Hold my hand so you can help me through.
But you don't stop to listen to my plea.
Oh please see me.
Please don't judge in silence

I will get my message heard
Parkinson's a scary word.
You can't catch it so should have no fear.
I can't ignore it as it's always here.
But my words into the darkness fell
And echoed around the walls in silence

And as the people stopped to stare.
Of my pain they're unaware.
So can't they see that I am falling?
Can't they hear me when I am calling?
And I know that the message from the people
Is they can't really help at all
So they let me fall.
As they walk away in silence.

Sue Hammond

Three years ago

Three years ago I thought my life was quite good
Apart from feeling stiff, a few falls and legs like wood
I'd put on a bit of weight, I knew I was getting old
It was either that or my age, that's what I was told

I was diagnosed with Parkinson's in the September
A month later my marriage was over, it hurts to remember
I can't help but wonder what I did that was so wrong
That my happiness should be taken, it's hard to be strong

Three years on the divorce is over the fight full of pain
Getting to grips with the Parkinson's pretty much the same
So I have moved from my home into a small flat
Getting ready for disability, now on my own I'm sat.

I get told I should be proud of the way I have coped
How I have got on with my life not stopped and moped
You are so brave they all say, you are so strong
If they only knew how much they are wrong

For the sake of my sons, I say I am quite well
But I'm scared and lonely if the truth to tell
Because you see I can't let anyone get to near
I face my future with a deep rooted fear

It is costing me much, because I have to pretend
Like I'm trapped in a nightmare that has no end
I'm buried so deep, don't know who I am any more
I am afraid of what my future has got in store.

Sue Hammond

It's time to go

My marriage had ended I was all alone.
I will have to fight the PD on my own.
I suppose this was how it was meant to be
Well at least one of us got to break free.

I've seen marriages, so happy and long
Crumble and fall as the PD grew strong.
So I had to warn you when first we met
Don't get to close for I'm not a good bet.

When we first met I knew from the start,
That all too soon we would have to part.
You need to know I didn't set out to hurt you.
I've seen the angst other couples go through.

I can see the end like a well-read book,
Although into the future I try not to look.
If you have to leave, don't take no blame.
I think that maybe I would do the same.

For now let's have some fun for awhile
Let's laugh and dance and put on a smile.
And eventually as the going gets tough
When you struggle and you've had enough.

I will know that you won't be leaving me
Just this horrible crap that we call the PD.
I will feel bad if you feel you must stay
So hold your head high and just walk away.

Sue Hammond

The Demons come at night

When I got PD I didn't know what to expect.
Though I knew it was something I'd have to accept.
So I decided to fight back, and take it on the chin.
I would keep fit and enjoy life. Even if I couldn't win.

I am strong, I am a fighter I have got a handle on this.
If you don't look too close you'll find nothing amiss.
Though I fight to keep moving, I'm doing okay.
I don't let it stop me doing things my own way.

I push myself on. I won't just curl into a ball
All things considered I'm doing alright overall.
My Medication works, most of the time.
And during the day I feel quite fine.

But in the night the demons come and the fear creeps in.
Then the "what ifs" send me into a downward spin.
I can only keep fighting this if I stay sane.
I get anxiety, I forget stuff, I don't feel the same.

I'm more afraid of the Meds than I am of the PD.
I've seen the changes it can make to your personality
I am aware of the compulsions that I may get
So all through the night the fear tightens it's net.

I awake feeling vulnerable and rather uptight.
I have been fighting demons for most of the night.
These thoughts are pushed aside during the day.
I send them packing and shove them away.

It's not something that I feel I can really share.
To worry friends and family would not be fair.
They all think I'm so positive and coping well.
And most of the time I am, so there's no need tell.

So from them this secret I will keep.
They don't have to know that I struggle to sleep.
I just need to tame these demons of mine.
So take a look at me, I am doing just fine.

By
S.C. Hammond

Betty Blue

Sometimes when help is needed help will find you.
This was certainly the case when I met Betty blue.
I was drowning in depression and couldn't get out.
But then along she came and fished me out.

I'd met her before, when I first got PD
Though I decided help groups were not really me.
But she left me her number, just in case.
So I rung her up and to my aid she raced.

She turned up at my home, this strong feisty blonde.
I thought she was someone with whom I'd not bond.
Then I found out she had come though she was ill.
That showed her kindness and a very strong will.

I wasn't coping with my new PD life
The negative feelings were just running rife.
But she got me fighting, right from the start
This kind friend with her big heart.

She pretends she's tough when people are near.
But her future's uncertain and holds some fear.
I see her vulnerability, it's there in her eyes.
Because like me in the shadows she hides.

So together we will stay strong
Helping ourselves and others along
She taught me that Pd isn't the end
I'm proud to know her, she's my best friend.

Sue Hammond

PD just keeps giving

Parkinson's plays dirty, it will kick you when you're down
It will keep adding to your symptoms, it really goes to town
It keeps giving you more ailments to add to your list
You don't know which ones you'll get, that is the twist

My problem at the moment may seem like nowt
But still in pain and frustration I will shout
As I rush to the loo with a burning pain
I have an infection attacking me again

As I get that familiar sting I can only weep
This will be another night without any sleep
I know what to do I have been here before
I get them every other month, sometimes more

I can read all the signs I have them often enough
I'll take antibiotics though they make me feel rough
PD likes to test us, pushing us more and more
Soon there will be more symptoms laid at our door

Sue Hammond

Where's our shining knight?

I asked the specialist to explain my PD
I believe knowledge is power, maybe that's just me
He said I would be turned off and on like an old radio
I thought how weird but he's the man who should know

He said you will know when you are going off
"Why, will I smell"? I asked with a smile and a cough
He just looked over his glasses at me all stern
Oh well I suppose I was there to learn
I didn't say what I thought about being turned on
He would have been out the door and long gone

Now I had my pills, my weapon against PD
From his grip for a while I would be free
But he was still there, he was having a good laugh
As my new pills had me dancing around looking daft

The specialist gave me new pills but where do I start?
From reality, me and my brain might well part
I could end up jumping some man for a sexual thrill
Or maybe steal money from out of the till
I could gamble or fritter my money away
Or turn to drink or do drugs every day

So come on you researchers be our shining knight
Give us better medication so that we can fight
If you give us the weapons then together we'll stand
We'll get PD out of our lives, and forever banned

By

S.C. Hammond

My Brain

When you're told there's something wrong with your brain
You know that your life will never be the the same
To be told that parts of your brain are just dying
Well if I say I'm not scared then I would be lying

I would rather lose an arm or even a leg
I'd just get a fake one and use that instead
If I had something not quite right with my heart
I'd make life style choices that would be a start

This is my brain that has gone badly wrong
But that's who I am, how can I stay strong?
As my brain struggles to give out the right code
My body's confused and goes into slow mode

Everyday hiding in the back of my mind
Is the hidden fear that only I can find
I try to fight it but it's always there
Sometimes, it's all too much to bear

As everything takes me so much longer
I know that Parkinson's is getting stronger
I try to collect my thoughts as I stand looking blank
I find a lot of things difficult now, if I'm being frank

So if you see me out, try not to judge
I'm still in here I just need a nudge
To collect my thoughts from a butterfly brain
You see I'm still me, just not quite the same

Sue Hammond

Did I sleep? I forget

I remember when I used to get eight hours sleep
I admit this new sleep pattern is making me weep
I have to say I've tried all the tips in the book,
But this insomnia won't let me off its hook.

You're at risk of Dementia with having PD.
So all the doctors are telling me.
The risk increases if you take a sleeping tab,
But this lack of sleep makes me feel bad.
Every night I curl up exhausted into bed.
But only get an hour or two to rest my head.

You risk Dementia if you don't sleep the doctors say
Oh dear, it looks like the Dementia will get me anyway.
Oh well if I lose my memory maybe I'll forget
That I no longer sleep, so I shall no longer fret.

Sue Hammond

Please don't judge

I need to tell you about a subject that's taboo
I don't know how to handle it, neither will you
Please don't dismiss me without a trial.
Listen to my words for just a little while.

I have been fighting the PD for twenty years now,
I try to keep fighting but no longer know how.
This hypersexuality has got its grip on me.
But that isn't the person I want you to see.

I spend so much time now on my own.
It's driving people away so I'm all alone.
I am trying so very hard to resist.
But the feelings are determined to persist.

I get empathy when I am out and my limbs freeze.
But this symptom just leaves everyone ill at ease.
I find myself apologising a lot of the time
These thoughts and feelings don't seem mine

I am feeling lonely and very sad too
Think how would you feel if it happened to you?
Can you please try not to judge? But look and see.
I know it's hard for you but it's much harder for me.

Sue Hammond

Uninvited Guests

I must tell you about the strange things happening to me
It started last week while I was just having my tea
A strange man in the corner of the room I did spy
He was staring at me, looking me straight in the eye.
I jumped from my chair, my heart filled with fear
I shouted "Get out, what are you doing here?"
Then bravado all gone I ran with a yelp
Around to my neighbours to fetch some help.
They searched my house from top to toe
They didn't believe me but he was there, I know
I think perhaps he was a burglar out to rob me
But then I caught him in the act so he had to flee

Then in the middle of night I had another scare
At the end of my bed a little girl was stood there
As I reached out to touch her she just disappeared
They must be spirits or Ghosts, should they be feared?
Then I realised, I knew what had happened to me
Of course it's not ghosts, just another gift from PD
You see it's not real it's all just my imagination
I have finally succumbed to the hallucination.
Now the uninvited guests are always around
They're hard to accept though they make no sound
If I go to touch them they will just slip away
But they always return, they're here to stay

By

S.C Hammond

Will I still be me?

The first poem I wrote was turned into a song.
But what if the message in it is all wrong?
I say in the end "I'm still me"!
But what if that's not how it will be?

Every night I lay awake as the dawn creeps in.
I'm writing poems when I should be sleeping.
I fall asleep but wake before it is light
As sleep eludes me night after night.

So another day dawns and I watch the suns rays
I have to break free from this foggy haze.
Fighting fatigue though in my bed I could stay
I must shake off the night and begin a new day.

So off to the gym I will go, to get myself fit
Exercising to music, lifts my mood for a bit.
I go to a singing class to help with my voice,
I'm not very good but that's my choice.

I do exercises to improve memory and mind,
But there'll always be something that I can't find.
Some days I feel just a little bit lost.
Fighting the PD is coming at a cost.

Everyday I seem to forget more stuff.
My mind wanders off. Enough is enough!
If the PD takes my memory then where will I be?
Because I'm sure I won't be saying "I'm still me".

Sue Hammond

I'm all shook up

So you think you know what's a wrong with me?
I'm slurring and a stumbling all around you see
The people are saying I've got the drinking bug
I trip up
I'm all shook up
Mm mm mm yeah yeah yeah

My body is aching and I feel really weak
I'm losing my balance tripping all over my feet
Who should I thank 'cause this Parkinson's sucks
I trip up
I'm all shook up
Mm mm mm yeah yeah yeah

I'm really hoping I don't lose my mind
My memory's so bad, but I say I'm fine
When the shaking starts I just need to rest
The Parkinson's too much it scares me to death

I sat up all night so no sleep I got
Insomnia struck. So in bed I'm not
I have to say that I wanna give up
I trip up
I'm all shook up
Mm mm mm yeah yeah yeah

My voice is quiet when I try to speak
My bodies so stiff that I feel like a freak
I wish there was a cure for this body of mine
But I have to wait for that cure to find

But I won't give up n I don't give in
Keeping up hope that one day we'll win
I get so tired that it's all too much
I trip up
I'm all shook up
Mm mm mm yeah yeah yeah
Mm mm mm yeah yeah yeah
I'm all shook up

Sue Hammond
Thanks Elvis

Dementia

The risk of Dementia is high with having PD
I'm told that this is what has happened to me
Really it's an excuse to have me locked away
So now I have to face strangers day after day
I am told that I'm here to be safe and at home
But it's no home when you're not free to roam
I plead with them daily to let me get back to my lad
But they don't care, wont even listen? I am very sad

They said today I'd see my son, but they lied
Just a strange man came and stood by my side
I asked him "have you brought along my son"?
He looked sad then said "can't you see it's me mum"
I got angry with him and I sent him on his way
It is cruel to mess with my feelings this way
He came back again with these sweet little kids,
But they're in on it too, they also tell fibs
The cheeky monkeys, calling me their Gran
What do they want? It must be some scam

I wish I knew why I had been sent here
My mind is all fuzzy and I can't think clear
The staff are friendly and really quite nice
But if I could escape I wouldn't think twice.
Then at the window, a frightened old lady I see
Can someone help her please, make her some tea
"Don't get so stressed" they say "it's just a reflection of you
You will be alright sweetheart your medication's overdue"
I'm so scared, everything's muddled nothing's as it seems
Then the pills kick in and I think perhaps it's all just a dream

Sue Hammond

Miscellaneous Poetry

By
Susan Hammond

Happy New Year

We welcome in 2019 with a shout and a cheer
But for me the old one I will shed a small tear
My eldest turned forty, the years just went by
Where did my life go? I ask with a sigh

I used to be young and exciting, a frivolous thing
Now no dancing on tables for me or a highland fling
No more wolf whistles seem to be coming my way
I'm afraid I am past my best, I've had my day

It seems I blinked and then became sixty
So now I'm officially old, it's such a pity
I'm over the hill with no memory of the top
Running down the other side so fast I can't stop

I should have been up there drawing my pension
But some jumped up little idiot added an extension
But now I've given up work, just to spite them
So I can put my feet up and potter in the garden

Please don't worry though it's not all doom and gloom
As there on the horizon my old age seems to loom
My sons are all grown, they are fine young men
And as their mum I am so very proud of them

I also have Grandkids so beautiful to behold
Though they'll always see me as Nana and very old
But I still get all their cuddles and kisses too
I have been truly blessed, I know that is true.

So now as I do the ladies that lunch
We are all a bit of an eccentric bunch
I put up my feet, relax in my chair
And write out some poems for you to share

Sue Hammond

Glasses and Pen

I need to write to my friend Jane
The diary says it's her Birthday again
I need to find my glasses, I have more than one pair
I know where they should be but they won't be there.
You see they like to lead me on a merry dance.
I won't just find them with a quick glance.

So it begins, the game of hide and seek
Into every corner I will have to peek.
They may be in the garden shed,
In the bathroom or under the bed.
You see they like to hide up really well
Where they'll be found I never can tell

Their friend the pen is just as bad
He thinks he's a real jack the lad.
And so the pen joins in with the fun.
And now he also has me on the run

We all know, take your eyes off a pen
That will be the last you'll see of it again.
You see there is a place where all pens go.
Where that place is we will never know

So now with pen and glasses in hand
At last triumphant, I can stand.
I have them for now but my head feels sore,
And I can't remember what I wanted them for.

So I sit down and rest a while in my chair.
But I know when I wake up they won't be there
Off they will go again having their fun.
Oh! They do like to keep me on the run.

Sue Hammond

Exciting and new

You met a young woman exciting and new.
You knew straight away she was the one for you.
With her you wanted to share your life
And very soon she became your wife.

The years went by, they just flew.
Your love for each other just grew and grew.
Life was good it was all on your plate.
You had her love, she was your soul mate.

As you got older, you and your wife,
It was all too easy, your comfortable life.
You wanted excitement and begun to feel bored.
So off you went and soon you had scored.

You met a young woman exciting and new.
Life was fun again and the excitement grew.
Then it unravelled when she wanted more.
But you still loved your wife, now you weren't so sure.

Your wife found out and now she has gone.
You're on your own, don't know where you belong.
You told too many folk, of your new lady friend.
So you broke her heart and it came to end.

Now as you stare back into the past,
A love taken for granted, could never last.
You want it all back, your old easy life
But she has gone, the one you called wife.

You both lead your lives now always apart.
It was beyond repair, her broken heart.
You'll find someone else exciting and new.
Now this story has ended for her and you.

Sue Hammond

The lake shore

As I walk my dog by the golden lake shore.
It's just five minutes from my front door.
I walk upon a carpet of golden leaves.
A gift from above floating gently down from the trees.
Some birds have left for climates warm,
But new visitors arrive with every dawn.

Too soon the cold of Winter I will feel.
Cold crisp air on my skin, biting and still.
I'll wrap up warm in hat, gloves and scarf.
I don't care if my bobble hat looks a bit daft.
Takes my breath away the haw frost hung tree.
Natures winter wonderland is waiting for me.

The first sign of Spring brings with it new life.
I can forget all my worries, troubles and strife.
As the low sun creates on the water a glare.
I marvel at the signets and ducklings there.
The trees are full of spring bird song.
All this I drink in as I walk along.

The Summer arrives and with it the heat.
The lakeside now full of new people to meet.
Families paddling with children carefree.
Paints a contented scene for all to see.
All this happens on the lake shore.
Just five minutes from my front door.

By

S.C. Hammond

The Menagerie

Come and meet the menagerie that lives inside of me
Firstly in my bonnet you will find lives Mrs Bee
Although you find it hard to see exactly where he's at
You may hear him flying past that will be Mr Bat.

So now then, who's up next? Ah, the playful Kitten
She's so cute and cuddly we can't help but all be smitten
That is except for grumpy Dog he's just having a moan
He always thinks that someone is going to take his bone

A pet has gone missing, which one it's hard to know
Though it must be true 'cause a little Birdie told me so
I open up my bag and out jumps a very angry Cat
But she won't go too far because she can smell a Rat

My mouth tastes awful, a bit like a Badgers bottom
Though I wouldn't miss him, he really is quite rotten
I have just had a check and I've still got my Beaver
So you see it's not her that has gone missing either

I often get told that I should keep my beak out
So that means Mr Duck is still somewhere about?
On the end of my tongue it feels like I have a Hare
So it is definitely not him, he's still stuck in there

I think I would remember if I'd left one with the vet
'Cause in my head lives Elephant and he would not forget
Ah, I should've known it, someone has really got my Goat
I found this out from Mr Frog who's been living in my throat

Sue Hammond

Parkinson's Poetry & Miscellaneous

Hubby

T1Tommy

ElleMac

JonB13

Neenag59

Jackson

Today I Cried For Me

Today I cried for me
I cried for my loss of dignity
I cried for all the things I've lost
The little things I miss the most

I cried for me and for my pain
For the things I'll never do again
I cried for legs that don't work right
For hours spent awake at night

I didn't cry for sympathy
Nor for pity that's not me
It wasn't anger, rage or hate
So why this sad and sorry state

Some things have gone forever
They won't return I know, not ever
I'm missing me I think that's why
I sometimes sit alone and cry

It's not my body, not my brain
It's not my fault but it is my pain
It's like I've gone been replaced
Even though it's still my face

What to do? I do not know
Put a brave face on keep up the show
This game of charades is now my life
It has to go on whatever the strife

So excuse me if I take a while
Lose the chatter, drop the smile
As I have a little cry just for me
Nobody will have to see

Life will just continue on
No different, nothing wrong
But when it's dark, too dark to see
I'll shed a few tears, just for me

Hubby

Unwelcome Friend

So my dark unwelcome friend
We'll be together until the end
I know you'll never let me go
Therefore there's things you should know

You'll try to break me, crush my soul
Push me into that black hole
Invade my dreams and make me weep
Twist my body and steal my sleep

You'll make me stumble when I walk
And make me stutter when I talk
My limbs may shake when I get bad
I might get angry even mad

But through the pain I will still fight
Every day and every night
You won't destroy me take my pride
I'll never run I'll never hide

So do your worst, I'll still be here
Laughing, smiling taunting fear
You may think I'm easy meat
A broken body a quick defeat

A damaged mind a broken heart
Just a shadow torn apart
You've got me wrong I won't give in
Even when I'm in a spin

We'll leave together when we go
I'll still be smiling this I know
So my dark unwanted friend
Listen to the words I send

Do your worst for I am ready
Even if a bit unsteady
I go to war with you each day
Take your blows in every way

And when it's time for me to go
I'll still be fighting don't you know

Hubby

No Angels Today

Someone, somewhere, can't you see
Today there's something bothering me?
I'm screaming at you can't you hear?
I'm scared, I'm frightened. Filled with fear

Isn't it showing in my eyes?
Surely you must realise
Every step is racked with pain
My feet are glued to the floor again

My head starts spinning round and round
I know I'm heading for the ground.
Stupid legs, stupid body, stupid brain
Nothings working once again

Passing strangers seem to think
That I've had too much to drink
I hear the whispers I see them stare
Their lives too busy to let them to care.

I want to ask but the words won't come
This doesn't feel comfortably numb
"Help me, I need you somebody please"
By now I'm sinking to my knees.

Grabbing at the unhelpful air
Maybe it's my manic stare
Can't they see that I'm so afraid?
Nobody's coming to my aid.

The concrete gives a familiar thud
First the pain then the blood.
Still they go on their way.
I'm on my own. No Angels today

Hubby

You Thief

You've stolen my strength, you've stolen my skills
You've left me with twitches, you've left me with pills
You've stolen my future, you've stolen my spark
You've stolen my smile. You've left me in the dark

You've taken my dexterity, you've taken my speed
You've taken my sharpness, all things that I need
You've given me stiffness dullness and pain
Aches in my muscles and fog in my brain

You've stolen so much you dirty thief
You've left me with anguish and grief
But understand this you evil disease
Though I'm damaged and down on my knees

You can't take my heart you can't take my soul
Whatever the agony whatever the toll
I won't let you beat me I won't let you win
I won't stop fighting I will never give in

So each time you rob me, take something away
I'll find a replacement a new game to play
So do your worst you bringer of tears
You stealer of dreams you thief of my years

I have got something you don't understand
It gives me the edge the ace in my hand
For I have love so deep and strong
For life and for living all day long

There's something in me you can't steal away
And I'm going to fight for it every day
So you sneaky thief you'll be back I'm sure
You may win some battles but never the war

Hubby

I'm Still Me

I know you don't know what to say
But don't just turn and walk away.
This past six months have not been kind
My body is different, so's my mind

Things have changed of course that's true
It might be difficult for you.
Accepting that I'm changing fast,
No going back. What's past has past.

If you can't look me in the eye
Then quietly leave. Just say goodbye.
If you can't handle me today
It's better that you walk away.

I need friends who make me smile,
Who give me respite for a while?
Friends who lift me when I'm sad.
I spend enough time feeling sad.

So while you're with me laugh and smile.
It's only for a little while.
In spite of what you think you see,
It's still me in here. I'm still me

Hubby

Mr. Sandman

Oh well here I am on the sofa again
With a few thousand thoughts disturbing my brain
The heating is off but I'm feeling quite cosy
With my Buzz Light Year duvet I should be happy and rosy
But needless to say that's just not the case
As the Demons in my head are having a race
I try to send my thinking down a different track
But the real bad thoughts always find the route back

I think of the past and future both on the same thread
At the same time wishing I was asleep in my bed
But what can I do I ask you my friend
When the Sandman won't let the alertness come to an end
At some point exhaustion will get the better of me
With any luck it will be during daytime TV

I don't want to suffer Philip and Holly
Or the mad antiques man who fakes being jolly
So come on Sandman I'm waiting wide awake
You kept me up long enough, so give me a break
It's about time you came back into my life
And let me sleep alongside my wife.
You are bad to me Sandman keeping me with your force
Will you not be content until my wife files for divorce?

T1 Tommy

Peppermint Gel

I thought it was an ordinary day, having a shower
However I could not have foreseen the green gels power
Peppermint fresh it said on the bottle, that was square
But absolutely no warning of washing down there

Scrub scrub scrub as I started to sing
But in a very short time I began to sting
Hotter and hotter it soon starts to be
"Time to escape" my bits said to me
You may be thinking his bits can't talk
Well something said abandon ship or you'll never walk

I'm now on the bus still burning but smelling nice
But I could really do with a big chunk of ice
I'm in real trouble now I'm stamping my feet
I put my bits out of the window as I stand on the seat
Things start to feel better as I begin to cool
But everyone's laughing and pointing at the fool

Thank goodness that I'm now at my stop
I walk past the driver 'n say "Back there needs a mop"
So take heed my friends with the peppermint gel
Don't do what I did because it's freaking hell
Be very careful and use it with care
Whatever you do, don't use it down there

T1 Tommy

Nobody's Phone

As I take my dog for a walk and he stops at a tree
I cross the icy bridge and go A over T
I lie there gasping and fighting to breathe
I believe that's my ribs poking through my sleeve
Oh well I'll have to be brave and do a few checks
Ooh thank God for that, it's only my specs.

It's time to get up and get hold of my mutt
But each time I try I'm back on my butt
Eventually I manage to get to my feet
Get my dog on the lead and give him a treat
I start my way home huffing and wheezing
Now I'm worried that I might start sneezing

If I do that it is really going to hurt
My ribs will be saying hi to the outside of my shirt
Although I'm in a world of pain and it's cold and sunny
And I'm sweating like hell but I still find it funny
I'm glad nobody's captured my spill
'Cause first thing they'd do is contact Harry Hill

T1 Tommy

Dark Clouds

Shake off the dark clouds for they're always there
Floating distantly feeding on your fear
Forming a dark band just beyond your sight
When you forget them they line up to fight

You don't stand a chance if you fight alone
They regroup always, your weapon a stone
Help is here, to hand, help with this great feat
Help to save you, these dark clouds to defeat

ElleMac

Caught

Bedtime comes too soon, past midnight
Nothing but the moon, shedding light
Through the glass windows, brightness shines
To pierce those dark woes, stood in line
Stood at attention, just waiting
For some kind of mention, inflating
Their spirits for once; sleeplessness
Meanwhile not a dunce; creepiness
Joins him to scare, this late hour
Whoever should fear this one's power?
On tiptoes he slides, shoulders taps
His chosen besides, he kidnaps

ElleMac

Parkinson's

This disease will progress, it will do its own thing.
It will stay by my side, circling round like a ring.
With eyes looking quite blank, looking lost and far off.
These eyes of mine notice loud sounds like a cough.

With eyes looking empty watering in the sun.
I stumble up the hill 'fore the suns day is done.
I return to find out if the sun did do well
But don't really care as my eyes with tears well.

I think of the future, of stumbling and great falls.
Tripping over my feet, while unheard are my calls.
My voice becomes softer, disappears in the wind.
Reduced to a shadow, I'm unseen as if binned.

The sound of loud coughing that continues non-stop.
Is heard now through weak eyes, as everything I drop.
As my world drops right down and lands splat at my feet.
I now see mayhem that each day that's now mine to greet.

The advice is to fight and never give in.
To give battle your all, a battle you must win.
But others do forget this disease will progress.
It will do its own thing- may as well be my guest.

ElleMac

Strictly Dancing On Thin Ice

A new partner to dance a Fandango
Legs tangle when I try to just Tango
Rumba in the style of having drunk rum
Shaking away to the beat of that drum

Dancing on thin ice but then I just freeze
Stuck in the moment until I move my knees
Freestyle as my body busts a move
In time with the Dyskinesia groove

Jazz hands with an arm that doesn't do swing
Robotic movements it turns out is my thing
The slow step has become the new Quickstep
Bradykinesia brings a new concept

So come and join me let's dance on thin ice
Belly dancing, I will need some advice
Take the floor with Parkinson's you can lead
Time for enjoyment that's all you need

JonB13

Ministry Of Shakes And Tremor

At the ministry you wait.
See shuffling and clumsy gait.
Is this the Ministry of funny walks?
A questioning voice squawks.

It is answered with humour,
Ministry of Shakes and Tremor.
Idea of Monty Parkinson
Holy Grail and meaning of fun.

Always look on the bright side of life,
Even when Parkinson's is rife.
Sit around the round table
Eat peas if you are able.

Gawain was so fearless in battle,
Scared his enemies with almighty rattle.
Caused by tremors inside armours suit,
Mighty warrior of repute.

Another fable the life of brain,
Tells how dopamine does drain.
But like a lumberjack I'm okay
Even when Parkinson's is on display.

Fear is one of Parkinson's missions.
As unexpected as Spanish Inquisition.
Kill your parrot to force confession.
Take your pills or shaky regression.

The Ministry of Shakes and Tremor,
Drafts legislation for this drama.
If you want the meaning to life,
Monty Parkinson's can cause you strife.

JonB 13

Lonely

Sometimes my life feels lonely, sometimes I just feel sad.
I sit and think.... if only, things shouldn't be this bad.
Some days are filled with tiredness others filled with pain
I've now come to realise no two days are the same.

Fatigue can come from nowhere and knock you to the floor.
And just as you think it's over it flattens you once more.
What do I have to look forward to, what has life in store for me?
What can help me bear this life and somehow let me free?

Acceptance of my illness and love from friends like you.
Understanding and kindness will really see me through.
Sometimes I feel embarrassed it's so hard to explain.
I used to love my life and work buts that's when I had a brain.

I moved away and left you all because I couldn't bear to see.
You all living life to the full, whilst decline was all for me.
I think I was rather selfish, I should have trusted you all.
That those who loved me, would not stand and let me fall.

I could have asked for help, I knew you would be there.
Pride and humiliation took its toll, I pretended I didn't care.
Now I want to say to you, each and every one.
Thank you for being in my life, you've all helped me move on.

So Parkinson's you listen!! I think I've got it right.
I'm no longer running, I plan to stay and fight.
A chance for a cure for Parkinson's everyday seems more real.
So I won't giving in too quick, I'll renew my fight with zeal.

Neenag 59

Morning

Well I went to bed at midnight
Every bone in my body aches
But I was asleep in minutes
That's all it usually takes
I woke at 5am I hadn't moved an inch
My goodness would I suffer now
As my stiff body ached and winced
Time to execute my plan I use when "stuck" in bed
Watch that I don't lean too far
And plant my face in the floor instead
First I start with "in bed stretches"
I try to arch my back
Ow ow ow blinking ow
I ain't doing much of that
I'm well and truly stuck you know
What the hell to do
I can't lie here for much longer
I really need the loo
Right go for it
Grab the bed side bar
Pull and grunt, cough n twist
You've done it, there you are
Shuffle shuffle moan and groan
Thank goodness I had a wee
I needed that more than you know
To make room for my morning tea
Medication taken, time to wait
I'll soon be dancing round the place
Two more coffees later
That smiles back on my face

Neenag59

Despair In The Night

I'm just sitting doing nothing 'cos I'm tired beyond belief
And my words are all slurry so the phones no relief
My arm aches, my hand shakes, my head hurts like hell
And my friends are out without me. I'm no fun truth to tell
I'm no fun because I stumble, I slur and I shake
And their pleas that I come along are lovely but fake

I'm no fun they need space from parents who are ill
And jobs that are demanding and teenagers they could kill
They want some me time and really I do understand
So I stay at home and check out 'Parkie Land'
Read and stay informed they say. Think positive, don't moan
Find a career, join a group. You can do this.... on your own

You can be fulfilled, be empowered, and live life to the full.
Do all the things that you enjoy don't mope and be dull
If you try just that bit harder you'll be better, you'll see
Who needs to walk and talk?....Clearly not me
It's not my reality; it doesn't resonate
So I sit here in the darkness pondering my fate

Take control? Be empowered? Dependency must end;
(In reality am I deadwood?- just not worth the spend?)

Jackson

Concluding Poem

After reading our poems, you may think what a sad lot
But let me reassure you that unhappy we're not
Despite the PD, most of the time we are alright
We're just vulnerable when sleep evades us at night

When you're diagnosed with a degenerative condition
Everything changes, putting you in a strange position
You need to adapt when there's less time with good health
We no longer feel the need to save to accumulate wealth

Released from these bonds, we have now been set free
We have to live life to the full while we can, you see
No longer waiting to retire to have a good spend
We have more time for loved ones until the end

I've met some nice people, who've become good friends
I know they'll be there to support me until the end
I find myself more patient and with more empathy
I now seem to be a better version of me.

I have time on my hands now I've given up work
I'm still quite busy, responsibility I do not shirk
I'm trying to raise money for that elusive cure
So please can you help, even if you're not sure

This illness can strike anytime, anyone
Father, Mother, sister or even your son
They don't know the cause and it is hard to treat
To find that cure would be amazing, quite a feat

Sue Hammond

Acknowledgements

I would like to thank

Hubby, TommyT1, Jackson, ElleMac, Neenag59 and JonB13

For letting me use their poems in this book.

Stacie Shorten

For the layout and design for the book cover

Mark Butler and Jenny Jones

For doing my proof reading

Ian Clarkson

For being my sounding board

Parkinson's Uk

For all of us in the UK suffering from this horrible condition.

Betty Blue

For being strong for me.

Parkinson's UK Information

Every hour, someone in the UK is told they have Parkinson's. Because we're here, no one has to face Parkinson's alone.

We bring people with Parkinson's their careers and families together via our network of local groups, our website and free confidential helpline. Specialist nurses, our supporters and staff provide information and training on every aspect of Parkinson's.

As the UK's Parkinson's support and research charity we're leading the work to find a cure, and we're closer than ever. We also campaign to change attitudes and demand better services.

Our work is totally dependent on donations. Help us to find a cure and improve life for everyone affected by Parkinson's.

Parkinson's UK
Free *confidential helpline 0808 800 0303
Monday to Friday 9am-8pm, Saturday 10am-2pm
Interpreting available.
Text relay 180010808 800 0303
(free textphone users only)
hello@parkinsons.org.uk
parkinsons.org.uk
*calls are free from UK landlines and mot mobile networks